A Gallery of
Berkshire Churches

Mark Chatfield

A Gallery of
Berkshire Churches

Mark Chatfield

Published 1974 Copyright © Oxford Illustrated Press
Printed by B. H. Blackwell, Printing Department,
Oxford, England
Bound by Kemp Hall, Oxford
Published by Oxford Illustrated Press, Shelley Close,
Kiln Lane, Risinghurst, Oxford

SBN 902280 20 1

Foreword

This book is an attempt, in word and picture, to portray something of the rich variety of a neglected county's churches. I use the word neglected because Berkshire's churches have never been in the forefront of architectural development, and also because books dealing with the subject on a national level rarely contain references to them. In the pages which follow, therefore, I have tried to redress this grievance.

My selection of subjects is obviously a personal one but, in making my choice, I have adopted three criteria as a yardstick. Firstly, I have included features which are important, artistically and historically, on a national basis. Secondly, I have included items which are either unique in England or especially characteristic of Berkshire. Thirdly, I have combed the county's churches for subjects which offer potentially visually interesting photographs. Inevitably, though, the final arbiter is always one's personal fancies and prejudices. I am, for instance, drawn especially to the little village churches, those simple nave-and-chancel structures hidden away in remote corners, unknown and seldom visited. They always appear to have more character and to be more appealing than the large, familiar and self-important major churches. I have given, I hope, full justice to the post-Reformation churches in the county. In how many books, for example, can one see photographs of Kennington, Pusey, or Ruscombe? They are all here, and more besides, in this little gallery. Some features which I would have liked to include are in positions impossible for photography without resorting to artificial lighting, and the latter is something which I have always eschewed, considering it hard and unsympathetic. No sculptor ever meant his work to be seen in such conditions. Yet there exist ample examples to photograph, more than could ever be put into a single volume, without adopting this atmosphere and character-destroying technique. Of course, soft or diffused lighting can create reproduction problems, and, in this context, I would like to thank Oxford Illustrated Press for their reasonable-ness and patience. They have been throughout most sympathetic towards my aims and what I am trying to achieve. The publication of a first volume is always a difficult hurdle and I am most grateful for their willing-ness to produce this book.

Mark Chatfield,
Faringdon,
Berkshire 1974.

To Janis

Introduction

Churches possess an uncanny ability to harmonize with, and indeed enhance, the landscape in which they are set. So universal is this characteristic that one almost feels it to be an indigenous one, an intangible factor speaking of something beyond the mere physical presence of the building. Each church appears to have been placed in its setting with the assistance of a painter's eye. In reality, of course, the formula for this concorde with nature is comprised of the building's outward form, the weathering of long years, and above all, the employment of local materials. For a building cannot do otherwise than become a component amongst a blended totality when its bones are made of the very stuff that fashioned the hills and valleys, the plains and combs. Additionally, the church tower or spire introduces a sense of place, of scale in time and space, and of familiarity. Despite the decline in religious influence, the church still remains the focal point of town or village, a phenomenon due as much to its physical presence as to anything else. If one bothers to analyse one's receptivity to the essence of a place, it will be recognized that this holds true. Most towns and villages are to this day dominated by a tower or spire, except for those larger cities where commercial greed has sought fit to create new skylines of slab-like, soul-wrecking impersonality. But out in the country, village after village is heralded by a tower perhaps just protruding above a circle of trees, or a spire breaking the monopoly of the sky.

In Berkshire, the finest piece of townscape–the view of Abingdon from the opposite bank of the Thames–is 'made' by the spire of St. Helen's Church placed asymetrically in the composition. As one descends from the Chilterns into the Thames Valley at Wallingford, Sir Robert Taylor's needle spire of St. Peter's Church announces the town's presence long before the latter becomes visible. Lambourn produces a different impression. Ringed by gently sloping downland, sometimes bare, occasionally tree-clad, the noble tower of this grand church appears to be the very raison d'etre for that tenuous lane winding its way up the Lambourn Valley from Newbury. Yet at Faringdon and Wantage, the equally large parish churches lie long and low and thus remain indistinct amongst the melange of houses and rooftops. And at Newbury, although the tower is conspicuous from certain points, one can wander about the town without being aware of the building's existence. Hungerford is similar to Wallingford in that, coming off the Downs, the tower rings a distinct note in the valley below. But Hungerford should be approached from the west, ie. along the Bath Road. From there the church appears on the right, low-lying amidst the water meadows of the Kennet, with the canal in front and the town grouping itself in the background.

Among the villages, variety of setting is infinite, just as one would expect it to be. Some churches, such as Cumnor, enjoy a key central position, while others, like Wasing, stand away from any building. East Berkshire possesses several private settings; churches placed in isolation from their villages. Old Windsor, tantalizingly concealed at the furthest extremity of a lane, is just one example. They come as a surprise in this busy commuterland. The classic English ensemble of church-and-manor house, on the other hand, occurs quite often in west Berkshire, though not as frequently as in some other counties. The locus classicus is Charney Bassett where

the pair make a splendid show when seen from the west; the church small, the house larger, and in the foreground the willow-bordered River Ock. Then there are Appleton and Fyfield, offering more broken groupings, or Hinton Waldrist and Longworth with trees effectively screening the house. At Buckland the large, austere church is backed immediately by the Georgian Gothic manor house, a felitious juxtaposition of the genuine and the sham. Again, a church might recline in the park of a country house, a setting of contrived elegance that cannot do anything but enhance the favoured building. Englefield is one example, looking as it does through a screen of conifers to a lake far-spreading into the distance. Surprise is not absent, either. A very good instance of the unexpected is Sulhamstead Abbots, where the simple village church appears quite suddenly at the corner of a lane, with a charming thatched cottage for company. And who would imagine that a tiny church, containing a fine medieval tomb, might be found in such a sparsely populated setting as Little Shefford enjoys, a church, incidentally, not even marked as such on the one inch ordnance survey map.

One could continue almost indefinitely, for each church is unique and its setting likewise. That is part of the charm which makes church exploration so compelling. But the churchyards also deserve our attention. The beauty of English churchyards is proverbial and those in Berkshire are no exception. In spirit, they range from the too-orderly and suburbanized to the unkempt and overgrown. Between these two extremes occur numerous churchyards carefully and lovingly maintained, even where grass stays uncut and graves neglected. Yet the mowing of grass has become a controversial activity. With today's massive chemical desecration of the land, churchyards are often the last resort of wild flowers, driven away from the fields by a ruthless agricultural machine striving to sustain a frighteningly overpopulated planet. The mowing of churchyard grass, if it must be carried out at all, should be approached with discretion. In any case, the cropped lawns of some churchyards can never be as attractive as the subtle varying length of uncut grass, with its admixture of flowers, patterns of light and the sound of an active (and beneficial) insect population.

The trees which embower the churchyards and which are instrumental in the creation of their special beauty, are also justly celebrated. The yew is the most familiar species, nearly every churchyard possessing at least one, sheltering the gate or perhaps the porch. A venerable specimen can be admired at Aldworth, an immense, contorted tree whose trunk is now bound with iron bands to prevent it from splitting. Tradition maintains that it is over a thousand years old, ie. considerably older than the church. Another yew that may well be as ancient, shades the porch at Didcot, its branches spreading far and wide in every direction, an umbrella in winter and a parasol in summer. At Waltham St. Lawrence, a yew planted in 1635 forms a lychgate of itself, its sinewy branches only prevented from brushing the ground by stout posts driven into the ground beneath them. But the most moving tree-church relationship, the most agreeable union of Nature and Man, occurs at Avington. There, the small, unassuming church nestles below a gigantic, dependable cedar. The contrast in scale and mood is tremendous; on the one hand the compact, soft-hued shapes of the building seen against a backcloth of trees, and on the other the sombre, crisp, almost two dimensional forms of the cedar standing clear against the sky. Equally moving and poignant is the solitary, mangled, ivy-clad ash tree at Winterbourne, its ragged verticals set against a broad horizontal plane of bare downland. Yet, in spite of all this, the most memorable churchyard is that of St. Helen's Church, Abingdon, with its three sets of almshouses, its railings and old-fashioned lamps.

Many churchyards offer fine views of the surrounding countryside. That from Hamstead Marshall, with its wide panorama of the Kennet Valley and the wooded dip slope of the Downs beyond, is undoubtedly the most exhilarating. From Ashbury one obtains a similar, but wider-ranging view across north Wiltshire and from Coleshill a gentler conspectus of that county. The differences are patent; the former basically an expansive, blue-grey distance hovering, ostensibly detached, beyond cottage rooftops, the latter an intimate cluster of cottage drifting and sinking into an enclosed landscape of rolling, tree-mantled countryside. The most rewarding views of the Vale of White Horse present themselves at Great Coxwell and Shellingford. Both stand upon ridges surmounting a landscape embellished with elms and overshadowed by the brooding mass of Whitehorse Hill. The long-drawn continuity of the Downs dominates the view from nearly every church in the Vale, sometimes receding, sometimes ascendant, omnipresent and strangely compelling. Conversely, from Childrey one looks north across the Vale to the less substantial crest of the North Berkshire Ridge and its one major accent, Farringdon Folly.

Berkshire possesses 148 churches whose frameworks preserve pre-Victorian features. The majority are, of course, medieval but the total also includes seven complete post-Reformation churches. Furthermore, amongst those of the Middle Ages, quite a number, too many in fact, are predominantly Victorian, incorporating a minimum number of genuine features. One is tempted to call them parodies, sad reminders of what once was. Somehow, it seems cruel and mocking to retain a window, arcade, etc., from a building that had stood for centuries only to be destroyed by some self-appointed advocate of Middle Pointed. Yet it is too easy, perhaps, for us to look back and criticize. One should not forget, either, that in 1840 many churches were little more than dilapidated, tottering wrecks. Drastic measures were, indeed, a necessity. However, one cannot help but feel that the intermittent patchwork operations of the Georgians were less bigoted than the full-scale restorations of the 19th century.

But the story of Berkshire's churches is not to be read in terms of restoration alone. There is much to satisfy even the most demanding connoiseur of original surface texture and medieval detailing. Churches such as East Hagbourne, Harwell, Hatford, Shottesbrooke, Stanford-in-the-Vale, Steventon and West Hendred retain absolutely genuine fabrics. So do many others, even where an odd window, etc., dates from a restoration. One cannot call, eg., Ashbury, or Besselsleigh, or Uffington anything but authentic; their impression is first and foremost medieval. Interiors relate a sadder tale, however. Few retain the once universal box-pews, three-decker pulpit, gallery, etc., the accoutrements of a Protestant faith. These homely, domestic furnishings were anathema to the Victorians' ideal of a medieval church; they were automatically and mindlessly cast out and replaced by uninspired pews and pompous marble pulpits. Yet several sets remain, in half-forgotten places. Hamstead Marshall and Besselsleigh hold first and second places, Bucklebury perhaps third. At Coleshill, the south transept is equipped with box-pews and a gallery, and Sutton Courtenay's aisles are also generously supplied with these cosy seats. The least restored interior is certainly Hamstead Marshall's, with its box-pews, pulpit, west gallery and Georgian chancel decor. West Hendred's interior is completely paved with medieval tiles and that is an event not only agreeably charming but also extremely rare.

In conclusion, let it be stressed once again that the attractions of Berkshire's churches are to be discovered amongst small, hidden things rather than the obvious or the famous. At Harwell, eg., the choicest feature is a tiny head half-concealed within the decoration of the sedilia. Similarly, the most beautiful carving in Ardington Church – a Green Man capital – is to be found in an odd corner of the south aisle. Despite the magnificence of Uffington, it is the emotional conflict between the Christian edifice and the Pagan White Horse on the Downs that stays in the memory. Fleeting images of prehistoric men who inhabited Uffington Castle, the Roman invaders, the struggles of the first Christians, of Alfred against the heathen Danes, are brought vividly to life by this one equation in space and time. Churches are, indeed, magnets of history as well as centres of architectural interest. Senses emotional, aesthetic and historical should be equally applied when visiting an ancient church. Without them a balanced appreciation cannot be realized. Much of this can only be experienced by personal visits; a book can tell only half the story. Thus is it with this volume. In the pages which follow, photographs and captions attempt to portray something of the richness, the variety and the beauty of church architecture and its allied arts in one of England's lesser counties. It is an attempt, I fear, that remains inevitably an aperitif; the banquet awaits those who will step outside the book's confines and explore for themselves.

1   ABINGDON: St. Helen–*The Mayor's Seat*. Dated 1706, this is the only seat of its kind in the county. The unicorn illustrated is one of two such figures (the other is a lion) seated at either end of the pew. They are beautifully carved, dignified but friendly. The pew front displays openwork foliage panelling and there is also a wrought iron sword-rest. The source of the style of all these components is Wren's City churches.

2   ABINGDON: St. Helen–*Mrs. Elizabeth Hawkins*. This figure of Mrs. Hawkins was sculpted in 1782 by John Hickey (1756–95) and is acclaimed as his major work. The design consists of a large standing wall monument of white marble with the figure of Mrs. Hawkins seated and reading. Her left arm rests upon a portrait medallion of her fiance, the Rev. Mr. Hart. In addition, busts of her parents, sister and cousin may be found here. The monument is an accomplished piece, successfully overcoming the compositional problems involved in grouping so many busts with the main figure. On sunny afternoons, strident glass in an adjacent window throws flecks of coloured light across the marble forms. John Hickey was born in Dublin and practiced in that city before coming to London in 1776. He was appointed sculptor to the Prince of Wales in 1786 but never fulfilled the promises implicit in such a lucrative post. Throughout his career he was bedevilled by drink and it is said that he died of alcoholic poisoning. Other monuments by him can be seen at Bushley, Worcestershire (1775), Tanworth-in-Arden, Warwickshire (1778), Leyton, Essex (1787), Barnes, Surrey (1787), Chichester Cathedral (1789) and Beckenham, Kent (1790).

3   ABINGDON: The Baptist Church. Built in
1841, and set back from the frontages of Ock
Street buildings, this graceful and striking
façade comes as a surprising interlude in the
otherwise traffic-battered houses of this now
dowdy thoroughfare. The façade consists of a
finely proportioned stuccoed portico with four
Tuscan columns, an entablature bearing a
triglyph frieze and a crowning pediment. This
purely Classical design is a major architectural feature of the town.

4 ALDERMASTON: St. Mary–*Capital of the West Doorway. c*1130–40. The delightful capitals of the re-set Norman doorway, always the main entrance into this church, are comprised of paired affronted doves. They are the only Norman capitals in Berkshire displaying representations of this symbol of peace. For over eight-hundred years they have proclaimed their message and the quiet of the churchyard now seems to reflect and to amplify this.

5/6 ALDERMASTON: St. Mary–*Sir George Forster and Wife*. 1526. Made of alabaster throughout, this is the most accomplished medieval monument in the county. The effigies are superbly carved, the small mourners or "weepers" on the tomb-chest even more so. One of the latter has crossed legs, an arrangement which connects the monument with that of Lord Roos (1513) in St. George's Chapel, Windsor. Both must have been made by the same sculptor, probably in the workshop at Burton-on-Trent, Staffordshire. There are eight weepers on each side, males to the north, females to the south, and the west end has two kneeling angels supporting a shield. Sir George's head rests upon his helm, his feet upon a buck. Lady Forster's head is supported by two pillows held by a pair of angels. At her feet a dog bites her gown. All these motifs are familiar but here they are executed with an added sensitivity.

7   ALDWORTH: St. Mary–*Label Stop of the South Arcade. c*1330–40. This comical little figure of a dog is one of two such carvings that enliven a visit to this downland church. They are not great sculpture but each is carved with an abandon that endears them to the onlooker.

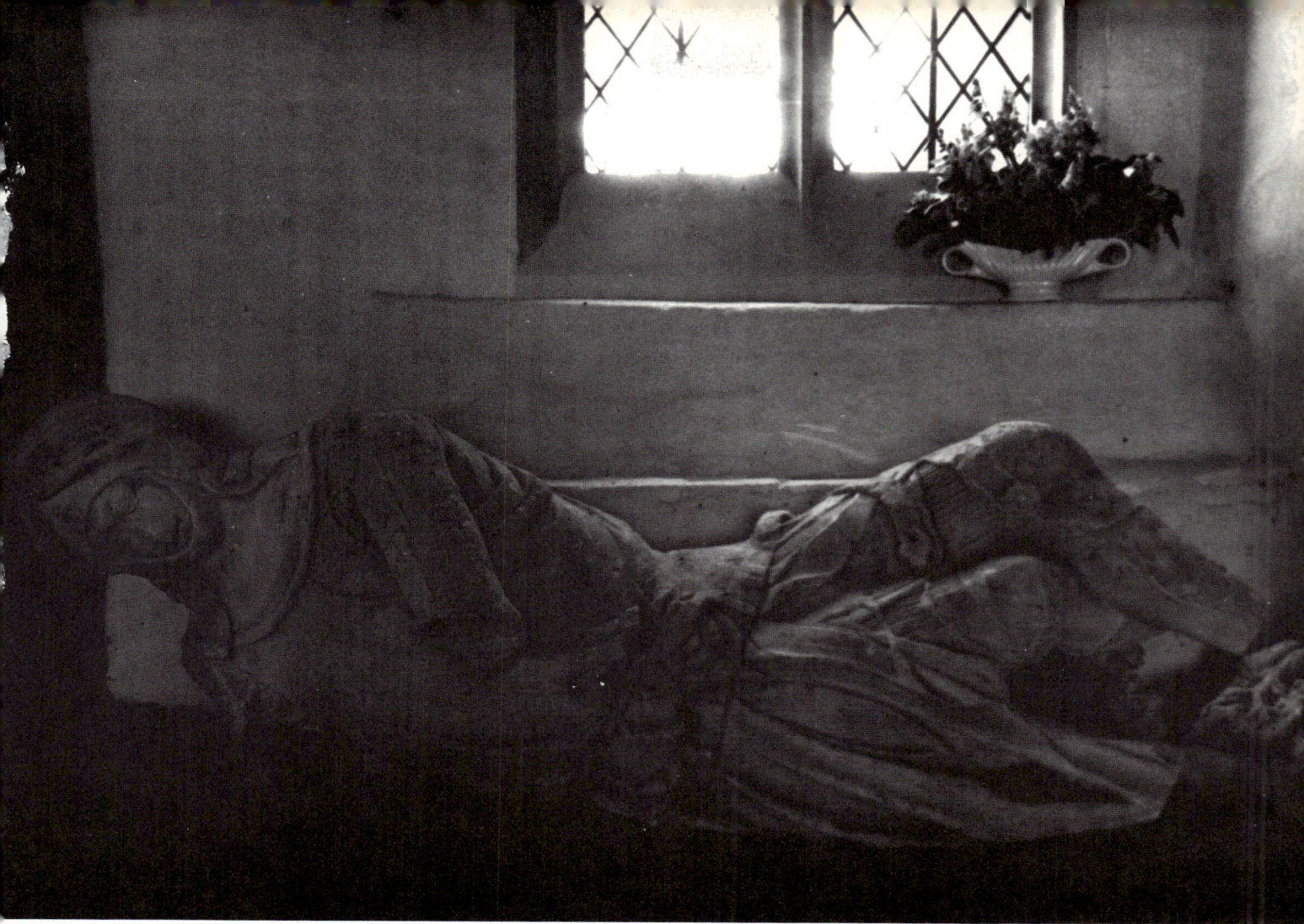

8/9/10 ALDWORTH: St. Mary–*The De La Beche Effigies.* The famous collection of nine effigies are known locally as the Aldworth Giants. The family came over with the Conqueror but died out in the male line during the 14th century. Queen Elizabeth I, on her way to Ewelme, made a detour specially to view their stony remnants. Battered and mutilated they remain an eloquent testimony to the wealth of this once great family. Six effigies lie under crocketed ogee canopies, three against the north wall of the nave, three in the south aisle. The remainder lie under the arcade. They date from *c* 1330–40 except for the two knights with uncrossed legs which are likely to be of *c* 1350. The other male effigies have, or had, crossed legs, a fashion which died out around the middle of the century. The most remarkable is that of Sir Philip the Younger (died *c* 1335–38). He is represented semi-reclining, an arrangement almost unknown in funeral effigies until the Italian Jacopo Sansovino popularised it in the 16th century. Here, the motif will have been taken over from manuscript illuminations of Jesse. The most accomplished figure is that of Sir Philip's wife Lady Joan, possibly the work of a sculptor from Abingdon Abbey. The photographs show (8) the south aisle with three effigies, (9) Sir Philip the Younger and (10) Sir Nicholas who died in 1348.

11   ARDINGTON: Holy Trinity–*Re-set Capital in the South Aisle.* Late 13th century and the most beautiful capital of any date in Berkshire. The head is a Green Man, one of those heathen folk deities (probably a nature God) wisely tolerated by the Church. Above, amongst naturalistic leaf, are a dragon and a lion representing Good fighting Evil. The development of naturalistic leaf began at Chartres and Amiens Cathedrals in the 1230s and first appeared in a mature form at Rheims from *c*1240 onwards. Westminster Abbey took it over from Rheims *c*1245–50 and it appears sparingly at Lincoln Cathedral in the 1260s. It reached its peak in the chapter house of Southwell Cathedral *c*1290.

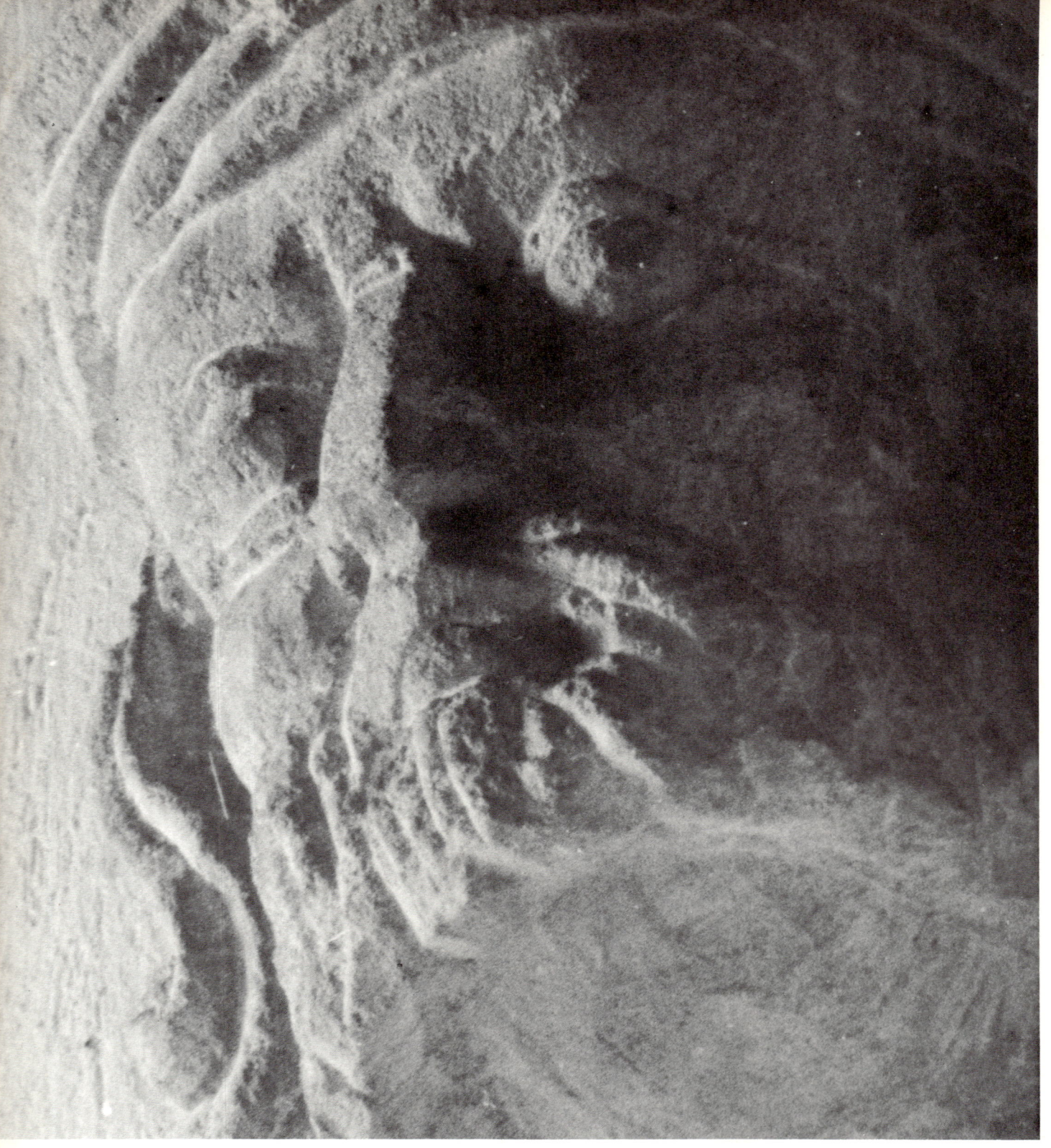

12 ARDINGTON: Holy Trinity–*Corbel of the Nave Roof.* Carved in the late 15th century, this corbel is just one of fifteen lively figures which peer down from the kingpost roof. Each is a spectator of the drama enacted in chiaroscuro between the west window and the dark recesses of the chancel. The iconography of these corbels includes two men with raised arms, six male heads, a bishop, two kings, a hound, a woman poking out her tongue and a dragon biting its tail.

13   ARDINGTON: Holy Trinity–*The Churchyard Cross.* 14th century. It was the practice during the Middle Ages to place a cross in the churchyard to commemorate the dead – the headstones with which we are familiar today came later. Not many crosses survive in a complete state (their sculpture was a target for iconoclasts). This is the only one to do so in this county. It has a three-stepped base and an octagonal shaft, the head of which displays four crocketed gables supported on tiny monsters. The wheel cross, however, may not be original. At North Hinksey the base and shaft of a cross survives but its head was destroyed during the Civil War. Stumps of crosses can be seen at Great Shefford, Hampstead Norris, South Hinksey.

14   ASHAMPSTEAD: St. Clement–*Wall Painting. c*1230–40. The most important set of wall paintings in Berkshire are to be found in this unassuming downland church. First to be seen along the north wall of the nave is a St. Christopher followed by a series of pictures from the Life of Christ and the Virgin. These depict the Annunciation, the Visitation, the Nativity and the Angels appearing to the Shepherds. Each scene is placed under a rounded-trefoiled canopy, an uncommon motif but one which occurs again at West Chiltington in Sussex. Above the chancel arch is a Doom, one of only two surviving 13th century representations of this subject (the other is at Patcham, Sussex). The figures of the main series are extremely slender, lithe and tender. The whole series may be the work of a painter from the Abingdon or Reading Abbeys or from a royal centre such as Windsor or Winchester. The photograph shows a detail of the Annunciation. Other Berkshire churches with wall paintings are Hampstead Norris, Padworth, Ruscombe and Stanford Dingley (13th century), Aldermaston, Baulking, Enborne, Kingston Lisle and Waltham St. Lawrence (14th century).

15 AVINGTON: St. Mark & St. Luke–*The Font.* c1160. This is one of the most mysterious Norman fonts in the whole of England. The iconography displayed beneath its blank arcading has never been fully or completely satisfactorily deciphered. The figure illustrated is obviously a bishop, one of thirteen figures set under the blank arches. The remainder cannot be positively identified, nor does there appear to be a set iconographical scheme. They are (going anti-clockwise from the bishop): a figure with head on lap (possibly St. Denis who was beheaded), a figure holding an object (possibly a key; thus St. Peter), a figure with arms raised (probably Christ giving a Benediction), a figure with hands on knees (possibly an archbishop), two figures embracing (almost certainly the Betrayal), a seated figure with arms crossed (St. Andrew?), two figures wearing capes and with hands on laps (possibly judges) and two figures one of which holds a circular object (possibly the Devil tempting Jesus). Some have thick pantaloon-like trousers while others have strange, boneless legs. The thick folds and the stockiness of the figures indicate the late Norman date.

16 BESSELSLEIGH: St. Lawrence–*From the South-West*. Surely the most charming church in Berkshire, stone-built, stone-roofed and with roses climbing the walls. The setting, too, could not be more favourable, even allowing for the main road only a few yards away. The churchyard is informal and picturesque with innumerable flowers, surrounded by noble trees and enclosed within a stone wall. To set it off there is parkland scenery in every direction. The church is basically Norman with later alterations which have retained the original humble plan of a straight-through nave and chancel. The interior still retains its original box pews and a painted tympanum instead of a chancel arch. The gatepier on the right is all that remains of the Lenthall's manor house.

17   BINFIELD: All Saints–*The Hourglass
Stand.* Probably of 1628 (date on the pulpit).
This, and a companion piece at Hurst (of 1636),
are the most elaborate amongst the hundred
or so surviving hourglass stands of England.
Both are of wrought-iron and so similar that a
common authorship can be assumed. The
Binfield stand is the most complex of the two
but both share many motifs. They include oak
leaf, grape and acorn and also animal subjects
such as a lion, a pelican, a wolf and dragons.
Much original colouring is preserved and the
animals, looking as if they were cut from
fretwork designs, possess a lively humour
entirely their own.

18   BISHAM: All Saints–*Sir Philip & Sir
Thomas Hoby*. 1558 & 1566 respectively. The
earliest of the three magnificent Hoby monuments in this Thames-side church. Of
alabaster and of a reticence strikingly
different from the grossness of later
Elizabethan tombs. The noticeably restricted
use of strapwork and the generally shallow
relief of the decoration accord rather with the
Early Renaissance than with the High
Elizabethan style. The figures are the earliest
post-Reformation semi-reclining effigies in
England and even more interesting is the
introduction of the relaxed position, a motif
which did not become universal until well
into the 17th century. Sir Philip's legs are
crossed and that is a deliberate imitation of
early 14th century effigies, a trend not
unknown during these years (cf. an even more
emphatically mock medieval effigy at Chew
Magna, Somerset). This most interesting
monument, the finest of its type in the
county, is a product of the Southwark workshop. Other standing wall monuments with
effigies can be seen at Little Wittenham (1611),
Pangbourne (1625), Tilehurst (1627), Radley
(1631), Ufton Nervet (1635) and Coleshill (1647).

19   BISHAM: All Saints–*Lady Margaret Hoby*.
1605. The most prominent and delightful of
the Hoby tombs and one of the most original
monuments of its date in England. It consists
of a high plinth reticently enriched upon
which stands a tall obelisk crowned by a heart.
At the foot of the obelisk sit four perfect
swans, their necks held back in graceful
S-curves and their wings spread out above. The
material is again alabaster with touch for the
obelisk. There is an almost exactly similar
monument (but without the swans) in
Westminster Abbey (Anne Harley) of the
same year and one is tempted to ask if both are
not by the same sculptor. Names, however,
are not recorded, which is unfortunate for this
monument, with its perky swans, is as
original as any by Nicholas Stone.

20   BISHAM: All Saints–*Lady Elizabeth Hoby*. 1609. This is the most sumptuous of the Hoby monuments, yet also the least original, being of a well-established type. The quality, however, is above average and the decoration is controlled and sparing. The kneeling figure, a Netherlandish motif, is the leitmotif of the composition. Altogether, there are seven figures, the largest being that of Lady Elizabeth herself. She wears a widow's hood (her husband, Lord Russell, having pre-deceased her in 1583), and faces a prayer desk in the familiar way. The background architecture displays ribbonwork and there is a canopy supported on Corinthian columns. An original wrought-iron railing surrounds the monument which is made, once again, of alabaster. Other Berkshire standing wall monuments with kneeling figures can be seen at Welford (1585), Abingdon St. Nicholas (1625), Tilehurst (1627), Hurst (1631), Radley (1631) and Buckland (1648). Kneeling figures occur also on many tablets.

21   BLEWBURY: St. Michael–*Flint Walling in the Chancel.* Flint is the characteristic building material of Berkshire's churches. It appears in 47 per cent of them, distributed across the central, southern and eastern areas of the county. Conversely, it does not penetrate further north than the twin villages of North and South Moreton, north Berkshire being a preserve of stone. Flint is an aesthetically indifferent material. In cloudy weather, or on hot summer days, it can appear lifeless and dull. It looks its best after rain, when its wet surfaces catch the light and glimmer in the sharp glow of a showery day.

22 BLEWBURY: St. Michael–*One of the Crossing Piers.* c 1190. This is one of a trio of Transitional crossings in the county, the others being at Faringdon and Lambourn. Blewbury is the smallest of the group but is important for its rib-vault. Vaulting in English parish churches is rare and that of so early a date even more so. Yet the chancel here is also rib-vaulted. Both vaults rest on corbels indicating that they were added as an afterthought. The decision, however, must have been made at once for the corbels display waterleaf, a motif of c 1170–90 which occurs also on the nook-shafts of the crossing piers. The photograph shows the north-west pier with the north transept beyond on the right. The piers are cruciform in plan, with slim nook-shafts adding vertical emphasis in the re-entrant angles.

23   BLEWBURY: St Michael–*Detail of the South Arcade. c*1200. Responds instead of piers indicate that the arcade was cut through a pre-existing wall. The capital in the foreground is an early form of still-leaf. It still retains something of Romanesque rigidity and the leaf has not yet freed itself from the bell of the capital. One ought to compare this capital with the later version at Long Wittenham (qv).

24 CAVERSHAM: St. Peter–*Headstone*. 1766.
This is representative of the many Georgian
headstones which add enjoyment to country
church exploration. They are the product of
village carvers working within well established traditions. The concentration of
decoration around the top of the headstone is
typical of such monuments in all counties,
though the material exploited varies region by
region.

25   CHARNEY BASSETT: St. Peter–*The Bellcote*. Early 17th century. An unusual and curious Jacobean feature, the only one of its kind in the county. The miniature parapet carries six obelisk pinnacles typical of their date. The larger embattled nave parapet is of the same time. This simple and very appealing rubble-built church is splendidly situated alongside the 13th century manor house. The pair form a most happy picture from the nearby bridge over the little River Ock. Willows frame the foreground and tall trees provide a backcloth. It is one of the best architectural groups in the Vale of White Horse.

26 CHARNEY BASSETT: St. Peter–
Tympanum from a Doorway. c 1100. Set up in the
chancel, this is the only Norman tympanum of
any value in Berkshire. It depicts a seated
figure between a pair of gryphons, each of
which bites the man's arms. Yet they are not
his adversaries; his hands rest upon their
necks and there is no sign of conflict. The
iconography is controversial. The composition
is supposed to represent the Flight of
Alexander (Alexander, wishing to fly up to
Heaven, entices two gryphons by holding meat
above their heads) but a passage from David
has been quoted. Alternatively, it may be a
representation of Daniel in the Lion's Den. The
composition is excellent, far more accomplished than that of many Norman tympana,
and may reflect a return to Anglo-Saxon
traditions. Judging by the quality of the figures,
the sculptor was decidedly more at ease with
animals than with humans.

27   CHARNEY BASSETT: St. Peter–*The Pulpit.* 15th century. This is the only surviving unaltered medieval pulpit in Berkshire. Its narrow panelling is enriched by a beautiful design of inset tracery. The top is plainly moulded. Altogether, it is a good example of functional village carpentry, executed without any desire for personal display. One further medieval pulpit survives at East Hagbourne but it has been extensively restored.

28 CHILDREY: St. Mary–*The Font. c*1200. Only thirty lead fonts survive in England and Berkshire can claim three of them. They are at Childrey, Long Wittenham and Woolstone. The first two are late 12th century, the third 14th century. This one, with its twelve regular standing bishops, is the most accomplished of the group. Each bishop wears his mitre and carries a crozier, the same mould being employed throughout. The font is a fitting companion to the fine collection of brasses preserved at Childrey.

29 CHILDREY: St. Mary–*Joan Strangbon*. 1507. Lying horizontally in her shroud, the brass has above her this beautiful Trinity; one of only two in the county (the other is also at Childrey, of 1514). God the Father appears at the top, God the Son at the foot, God the Holy Ghost represented as a dove in the centre. The head of the Father is especially beautiful, hierarchical yet tender. Amongst the late medieval brasses of Berkshire this is an outstanding piece. Many brasses of this date are of poor workmanship and fussy in their attempt to introduce shading and other three-dimensional effects. The Strangbon figure is an exception. Shroud brasses also exist at Longworth (1498), Childrey (1516) and Appleton (1518).

30 CHOLSEY: St. Mary. One of Berkshire's most impressive churches, this large cruciform building enjoys a commanding position on rising ground some distance north of the village. Architecturally, too, it is of outstanding interest. The crossing tower belongs to the Saxo-Norman overlap (c 1070), displaying Saxon masonry but resting upon early Norman crossing arches. A surviving window in the north transept, built at the same moment, is early Norman also. The beautiful chancel is perhaps the finest of the Early English period in Berkshire. It has internal shafting and an east window whose geometrical tracery establishes a completion date of c 1275. Although this window is an excellent example of first-generation bar tracery, the centre light pushing up against the main circle is indicative of a growing restlessness which eventually produced the Decorated style.

31 COMBE: St. Swithin–*The Bell Turret. c* 1500. The turret is of a type associated with the churches of Essex, ie. free-standing and with aisles. As in many Essex examples, there are aisles to north, south and west. They have lean-to roofs and then the turret proper begins, terminating in a pyramid cap. Shingles provide the external cladding. Internally there are four uprights strengthened by tie-beams, arched braces and scissor braces. These, however, are now concealed behind plaster walls inserted when the turret was converted into a vestry. Bell-turrets of the more familiar kind, placed upon the roof and supported from below by an internal timber structure, survive in original condition at Ashampstead, Didcot, Stanford Dingley, Swallowfield and Wasing.

32 COMPTON BEAUCHAMP: St. Swithen–
The Exterior from the North. This small church,
standing upon the Greensand shelf below the
Downs and above the Vale, is one of the most
picturesque in Berkshire. The exterior is
especially memorable, with its clean chalk
surfaces, irregular elevations and the
ludicrously tiny tower capped by a pyramid
roof. The building's setting is equally
unmatched and in Autumn, when the late sun
throws a flush of rose pink across the walls
and burnishes the copper trees behind, it
reaches new heights of beauty. Basically early
13th century, the Decorated and Perpendicular periods have added their own contribu-
tions without changing the scale. The roofs
are of stone slates.

33 COOKHAM: Holy Trinity–*Sir Isaac Pocock*. 1810. This sculpture is by John Flaxman (1755–1826) and is considered to be one of his finest works. The design possesses an intangible ethereal quality, an effect due to the placing of the figures and the swirls of drapery. Sir Isaac, who was drowned in the Thames, expires in his niece's arms. The couple are linked shoulder to shoulder by a drapery whirl and their heads, the expressive climax of the composition, are thus contained and given an heightened emotional intensity. The carving is of the highest quality. John Flaxman, England's leading Neo-Classical sculptor, was employed first by Wedgwood making drawings for pottery. He was in Rome from 1787 to 1794 and became a Royal Acadamician in 1800. His style is characterised by a strongly expressed linear technique, often of a rudimentary nature. Monuments by him can be seen in many churches. In Berkshire one can enjoy his hand also at Shrivenham (1800), Basildon (1804), Reading St. Mary (1809) and Hurley (1810). His Pocock tablet is beautifully lit by a soft directional light, drifting across from the north chapel east window.

34　CUMNOR: St. Michael–*The Staircase.* Dated 1685. Instead of the usual ladder or stair-turret, Cumnor's tower contains this unusual, but very fine, spiral staircase. It rises in four twists up to the ringing chamber and is still to be found in its original condition. Being a local carpenter's job, the motifs are out-of-date for 1685. The turned balusters, especially, are essentially Jacobean in style.

35 CUMNOR: St. Michael–*One of the Poppyheads in the Chancel.* Early 16th century. The ten poppyheads here are the best in the county. The illustration depicts two addorsed seraphims standing upon dragons' heads. Other motifs include shields with the Instruments of the Passion, chameleons, two heads and much leaf. The stall ends themselves are plain and have buttress-shafts. Poppyheads on benches or stalls survive also at Aldworth, Childrey, Cholsey, Clewer, Hurley, Long Wittenham, Reading (St. Laurence), Sunningwell and Wantage.

36   DENCHWORTH: St. James–*Corbel of a Bishop*. Early 15th century. The corbel, now battered by the effects of several centuries' weathering, is placed above the south-east buttress of the chancel.

37   DRAYTON: St. Peter–*A Detail of the Reredos.* Early 15th century. Illustrated is a detail of the Annunciation panel. This is one of six alabaster panels portraying scenes from the Lives of Christ and the Virgin. The others are the Assumption, the Adoration of the Magi, the Betrayal, the Scourging and the Entombment. These alabaster panels were produced in Nottinghamshire and put together to form reredoses, etc. to order. They were intended to be painted and some of the original colouring remains on this set. Considering how few are the surviving examples of these once numerous furnishings, this one at Drayton ought to be counted as a precious possession amongst Berkshire's medieval relics. It is, indeed, the only one of its kind in the county although another exists at Yarnton, Oxfordshire.

38   ENGLEFIELD: St. Mark–*Image Bracket. c* 1210–15. This beautiful piece displays three bands of characteristic Early English decoration. At the top is a row of finely cut dogtooth, a motif which is, in effect, a hollowed-out pyramid. In the centre, joined petal to petal, is a band of rosettes and, below, the stiff-leaf pattern is arranged in an alternating up-and-down rhythm. There is more good Early English work in this otherwise mainly Victorian church. The south aisle was allowed to remain and retains its excellent arcade and east window.

39, 40 & 41 FARINGDON: All Saints–*The Crossing & Arcades. c* 1190–1200. The arcades and crossing of this large and
impressive church, are among the finest work of any period to be found in the county. They are refined and disciplined
and the details are impeccable. Their blending of Romanesque and Gothic motifs form a perfect textbook of Transitional
architecture. The photographs show (39) part of this north-west crossing pier (40) a detail of the south arcade with one of
the clerestory windows beyond and (41) one of the corbels of the west responds. The corbel is an interesting two-tiered
version of early still-leaf, large-scaled and a little clumsy. That on the capital of the arcade is more controlled. The shafts
of the crossing pier displays a late version of the waterleaf capital (on the left) alongside another variety of early still-leaf.
The latter is of a freer design than the others, indicating a slightly later date.

42 FARINGDON: All Saints–*Detail of the South Door*. Early 13th century. One of the finest medieval doors in Berkshire, rivalled, perhaps, only by the slightly later example at Uffington (qv). The decoration consists of restless ironwork with many scrolls and several terminations in the form of open-mouthed dragons' heads. One of the latter is illustrated. Besides Faringdon and Uffington, medieval doors bearing enriched ironwork are preserved at Buckland and Frilsham (Norman), Hampstead Norris, Kingston Lisle and Sparsholt (Transitional), Blewbury and Stanford Dingley (Early English) and Didcot and Lockinge (Decorated). Later doors replaced ironwork by wooden tracery designs.

43   FYFIELD: St. Nicholas–*Sir John Golafre*. 1442. This gruesome effigy is of a type known as a cadaver, created in France *c* 1400 (eg. Cardinal de Lagrange, 1402 at Avignon). It first appeared in England at Lincoln Cathedral with the date of death 1431 (Bishop Fleming). So the Golafre family was fully up-to-date in its commissioning of this macabre form of memorial. The cadaver lies on the lower floor of a two-tiered tomb. On the upper tier is a conventional effigy in plate armour. All parts are of freestone and the cadaver is the only one of its kind in Berkshire.

44   GREAT SHEFFORD: St. Mary–*The Tower. c* 1200–10, the top stage *c* 1300 (cusped Y-tracery). The first date is correct, judging by the extant details, but they may represent the reconstruction of a yet earlier tower. This is the only surviving original round tower in Berkshire, though a rebuilt one exists at Welford further down the Lambourn Valley. There was formerly another at Shaw. The origin of round towers has aroused a great deal of controversy. The earlier ones may have been defensive structures but it is more likely that the circular plan was a necessity in areas lacking good stone for quoins. Certainly the majority occur in counties away from freestone sources (Norfolk 119, Suffolk 41, Essex 8) and it is significant that those in our county are to be found in the Downs which also lack freestone.

45 HAMSTEAD MARSHALL: St. Mary–*From the West.* This church stands upon a ridge commanding a wide view northwards over the Kennet Valley. It is surrounded by many fine trees and wild flowers are plentiful amongst the tall grass. Prominent in the photograph is the red brick tower, built in 1622 and which is representative of the eighteen Berkshire towers constructed of this material. The interior is the least restored church in the county (even less disturbed than Besselsleigh), having managed to preserve its west gallery, box pews, two-decker pulpit and Georgian chancel decor. Beyond the churchyard wall stand a pair of majestic gatepiers, forlorn remnants of the great house that once stood close by.

46 HAMSTEAD MARSHALL: St. Mary–*The North Aisle West Window. c* 1350. A beautiful, mellow design demonstrating the transition in window tracery from Decorated to Perpendicular, something not often seen. Old and new motifs are kept felitiously apart. At the top are characteristic reticulated tracery units, below this, instead of repeating it, the mason introduced Perpendicular panel tracery. This, and the corresponding east window, are the only examples in Berkshire, of this mixing of two motifs from two different periods.

47　HARWELL: St. Matthew–*The Tower. c*1250. Of the twenty Early English towers of Berkshire, this is decidedly the most personal. It is of three stages, the lowest with angle buttresses and the uppermost with nook-shafts set into the corners. The parapet is later. The windows have consistent plate tracery, providing a clue to the date. This form of tracery, the precursor of bar tracery, consisting of patterns cut into the solid stonework, is seldom found. It originated in the Ile de France about 1150 (Noyon Cathedral, etc.) and reached England *c* 1180 (Ripon Cathedral). In parish churches it belongs to the mid-13th century. Other Berkshire churches with plate tracery are Combe, Compton, East Ilsley, Letcombe Basset, Little Coxwell, Sparsholt, White Waltham and Woolstone.

48   HARWELL: St. Matthew–*Corbel in the Chancel. c*1310. One of the most joyously alive pieces of sculpture in any Berkshire church. The splendid, jocular little figure clutching a bottle sits against the rere-arch of the priest's doorway. His pose is a most awkward one and his head, displaying an appropriately silly smile, rests upon his hand. He is obviously drunk and thoroughly enjoying himself.

49   HARWELL: St. Matthew–*One of the Sedilia Hood-Mould Stops. c*1310. A sweet, lyrical carving of a woman's head, small (approx. two inches high) and self-effacing but one of the best of its kind in the county. She wears a wimple and is one of three heads on the sedilia. They, the corbel illustrated in the previous photograph, and the figure capitals of the chancel arch, combine to make this one of the most rewarding Decorated chancels in Berkshire.

50   KENNINGTON–*The Old Church*. Built in 1828 by Daniel Robertson of Oxford, this church is an early example of the Neo-Norman style which became popular during the 1840's. It is not, however, the first of its kind. The year before Robertson had designed St. Clement's, Oxford, also in Neo-Norman, but a less successful building than Kennington. Much earlier, in 1815, Henry Hakewill chose this style when he rebuilt Old Wolverton Church, Buckinghamshire. Kennington is particularly successful, because the scale is kept small and it is not used as a vehicle for ostentatious display. The building consists of a single-cell nave and chancel and a bellcote above the west gable. The west doorway is an exceptional piece of Norman imitation work. Other Neo-Norman churches in Berkshire are Hermitage (1835), Reading St. James (1837–40 by Pugin), Shaw (1840–42 by J. Hansom) and Burghfield (1843 by J. B. Clacey). The majority of these however are not as successful as Kennington.

51　LAMBOURN. A major church, perhaps the grandest in the county. In its valley setting of rolling downland, this splendid cruciform building assumes the dominance of a cathedral. The photograph portrays a close-up from churchyard level. Nave, transepts, crossing and the tower's lower stage are Transitional work of *c*1190–*c*1200. In the tradition of cathedral development, chancel and adjoining chapels were added or rebuilt during the 14th and 15th centuries. The Perpendicular bellstage of the tower is a particularly beautiful example of its date and harmonizes perfectly with the amazingly severe earlier parts below. In the gable of the west window is a circular window, not a common feature in England. The main west window is an early Perpendicular version of Decorated reticulated tracery.

52   LAMBOURN: St. Michael–*Sir Thomas Essex & Wife*. 1558. Renaissance motifs entered Berkshire's churches later than in most counties around London. The earliest case is that of the monument to Sir Thomas Unton at Faringdon where the date of death is 1533. That work is of a similar design to the Essex tomb illustrated here both coming from one of the Burton-on-Trent workshops. The sculptural standards of these workshops became less and less accomplished as the 16th century progressed and eventually succumbed to competition from Southwark. Although the Essex tomb is quite an eloquent work of art, the eventual decline of the Burton workshops formed a sad end to a tradition that had produced such fine monuments as Sir George Forster's at Aldermaston. The tomb-chest displays four panels divided by thin balusters, the panels with shields and vase-carrying angels, all typical Early Renaissance motifs.

53   LETCOMBE BASSETT: St. Michael–*Capital of the Priest's Doorway*. *c*1100. The most interesting Norman capitals in Berkshire. They display the four Signs of the Evangelists, two to each capital. The one illustrated here is the Eagle of St. John, the others being the Lion of St. Mark, the Angel of St. Matthew and the Ox of St. Luke. The carving is primitive but, in this unexpected location, is possessed with an expressive presence of no mean power. It is believed that this is the only priest's doorway in England carrying representations of the Evangelists' symbols.

54 LETCOMBE BASSETT: St. Michael–*One of the Churchyard Tombs.* Dated 1690. Berkshire's churchyards do not contain a great number of these big tombs and this is perhaps the only really worthwhile one of its date. But it is characteristic of many which can be found in most counties and more especially in the Cotswolds. The top has skulls set against shell niches and the sides are enriched with garlands. Buscot, Chaddleworth and Coleshill are also worthwhile churchyards for the tomb seeker.

55   LITTLE COXWELL: St. Mary–*The South
Side*. This small church, with its rendered
walls and stone slated roofs, presents one of
the most satisfying exteriors of any Berkshire
church. The plan is basically the original one of
c 1200 with later insertions and additions
(Early English bellcote, Decorated and Perpendicular windows, Perpendicular south
porch). Hidden behind cottages towards the
east end of the village, the church is
approached via a path that winds between
cottages and garden walls. The churchyard is
pleasingly sylvan with pretty, tree-framed
views across rolling landscape.

56   LITTLE COXWELL: St. Mary–*The Bellcote. c*1260. This is the earliest of Berkshire's three medieval stone bellcotes, the others being at Besselsleigh (qv) and West Challow. The structure contains openings for two bells and in the gable is a plate tracery quarterfoil. All surfaces are genuine and unrestored.

57   LITTLE SHEFFORD–*Sir Thomas
Fettiplace & Wife.* 1442. A poignant monument
in the most moving interior with which I am
personally familiar. Disused but not forgotten,
as the flowers on the dusty altar indicate,
plaster peels from the walls and the feet tread
upon a mouldy carpet. In the minute south
chapel, built by John Fettiplace to 'enclose my
father's tomb', stands this alabaster monument with its recumbent effigies and shield-
bearing angels. The loneliness of the figures,
the neglect, the peace and the warmth of the
sun create an emotive atmosphere unmatched
anywhere. The tomb is one of three such
alabaster monuments in Berkshire, the others
being that of Sir William Fitzwarin (1361) at
Wantage and Sir George Forster (1526) at
Aldermaston (qv). The effigies are small in
scale and finely detailed, more sensitive than
the majority of 15th Century examples. His
head rests upon a helm, his feet upon a lion. Her
head reclines upon a pillow supported by the
usual angels and her feet rest upon a hound.
Alabaster first appeared *c* 1330 (Edward II in
Gloucester Cathedral; John of Eltham, 1337, in
Westminster Abbey) so the Fitzwarin tomb
can be considered an early instance of its
use. The material, which is a crystalline
gypsum, was quarried extensively in the
Trent Valley and many workshops sprang up
in the area, especially at Nottingham. The
Fettiplace tomb was made in the workshop of
Thomas Prentys and Robert Sutton,
Chellaston, Derbyshire.

58 LONG WITTENHAM: St. Mary–*The South Porch. c*1340. This is an interesting example of one of Berkshire's six timber porches. It is a delightful piece, absolutely genuine from ground to roof and constructed of old weathered oak. The simple entrance supports a beam and the bargeboard above preserves the happy motif of ogee cusping. The latter even have subcusps. Plain balusters of square section carrying moulded capitals range along the open sides. Aston Upthorpe, Besselsleigh, Binfield, Blewbury and West Challow (qv) are the other churches with timber porches.

59   LONG WITTENHAM: St. Mary–*The South
Transept South Window. c* 1280. An interesting
design which displays the gradual move away
from the purity of first generation bar tracery.
The trefoiled lights are still of equal height but
the mullions continue upwards as sub-arches
splitting the tracery into three parts. This
tends to negate the unity of the composition.
In addition, the trefoils above the side lights
are no longer enclosed by circles. All these
motifs represent a first step towards the wilful
tracery designs of the Decorated period.

60   LONG WITTENHAM: St. Mary–*Capital of the South Arcade. c*1240. This is an example of later stiff-leaf and ought to be compared with the earlier variety at Blewbury (qv). Now the leaf has freed itself from the bell and has begun to spread diagonally around the capital. The carving has something of the quality of a braken frond. Sometimes the name "wind-blown" is given to this looser style of stiff-leaf.

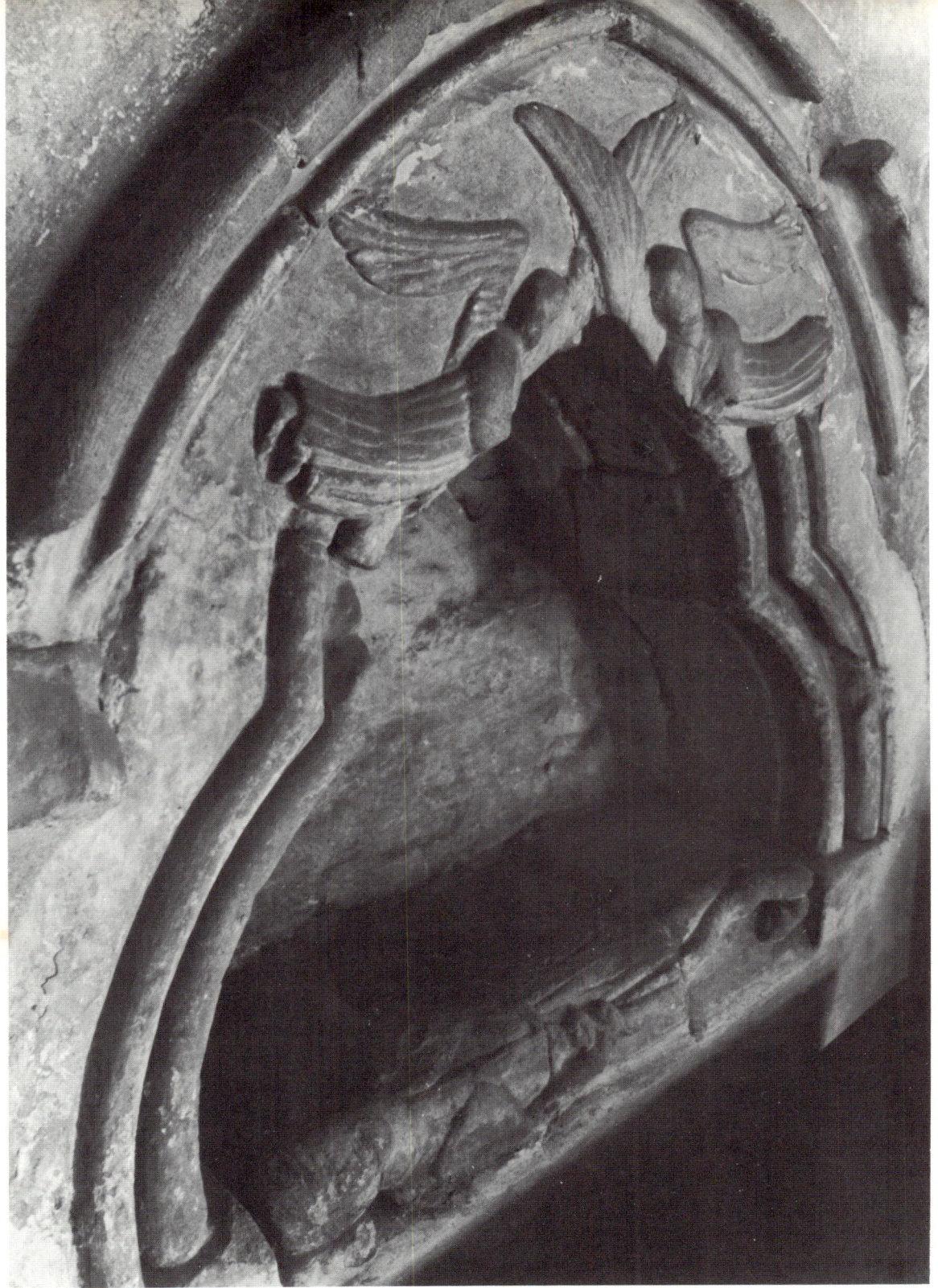

61   LONG WITTENHAM: St. Mary–*The Piscina-Monument. c* 1280. Unique in England, this remarkable feature combines the functions of a piscina and a memorial. The top foil of the moulded arch is concealed by two flying angels whose wings rise up and cross at the apex. At the foot lies a miniature recumbent effigy of a knight, his legs crossed. This is reputedly the smallest effigy in the country (24 inches). The angels are dainty, vigorous figures and, judging from the position of their arms, were probably censing. Their style may derive from Westminster Abbey.

62   LONG WITTENHAM: St. Mary–*The Font. c*1190. The second of Berkshire's trio of lead fonts. It is divided horizontally into two bands, the upper with wheels and rosettes haphazardly arranged. The lower band is comprised of thirty identical miniature bishops, each one under a blank pointed arch. During the Civil War the font was protected by a wooden case which now serves as a table in the south aisle.

63   LONG WITTENHAM: St. Mary–*The Font Cover*. Early 17th century. There are twelve of these Jacobean or Carolean font covers in the county, some plain, many decorated as here. Dated examples occur only at West Hendred (1630) and Abingdon St. Helen (1634). This one is enriched with arabesque executed in large S-shaped patterns. Arabesque decoration, the leitmotif of early 17th century woodwork, occurs on nearly all the font covers and pulpits of this period in Berkshire.

64   LONGWORTH: St. Mary–*Detail of the Chancel Screen.* Early 17th century. One of only three Jacobean screens in Berkshire, the others being at Long Wittenham and Kingston Lisle. Round-arched one-light divisions with turned balusters and a top cresting of strapwork. The crowning motif is a scallop shell. Strapwork was invented by Rosso Fiorentino at Fontainebleau in the 1530s. It was taken up immediately in Belgium and came to England soon afterwards. "Sursum Corda" means "Lift Up Your Hearts".

65 & 66   NEWBURY: St. Nicholas. Berkshire's major Perpendicular church and the only one which can stand comparison with those at East Anglia or the Cotswolds. It was rebuilt *c* 1509–32 by the wealthy clothiers of Newbury, the nave by John Smallwood, better known as Jack of Newbury. The plan is the typical one of west tower, nave with clerestory, aisles, chancel and chancel chapels. The latter are smaller in girth than the aisles and so the straight-through arrangement of the West Country does not occur. All parts are consistently embattled. The building's crowning glory is its tower, a tall, strong design with a flourish of crockets and pinnacles. The photographs depict (65) the exterior from the east and (66) the tower. In the former the silhouette in the foreground is that of the Gothick churchyard gateway.

67   NORTH MORETON: All Saints–*The South Chapel Piscina. c*1310. The highlight of the sculptural features in the chapel which was founded as a chantry in 1299. Ogee arches indicate a post-1300 date. The hood-mould is studded with ballflower and below it an ogee vesica is sunk into the angle, supported by a free-standing shaft. Angle piscinae are uncommon in Berkshire although there is a good Early English example at Baulking. A piscina, wherever it occurs, indicates the position of a medieval altar.

68 PUSEY: All Saints–*The Exterior from the South. c* 1745. An unusual and attractive Georgian building of stone, Pusey church stands at the east end of the village, between cottages and the grounds of Pusey House. Its architect is unknown. The exterior is austere with just an assemblage of cubic shapes under flat roofs. The bell-turret was added *c* 1840 in the Italianate taste. The plan consists of nave, north and south transepts and a short sanctuary. Victorian additions are thankfully absent (many Georgian churches have been ruined by lengthy 19th century chancels, Gothicized windows, etc.).

69   PUSEY: All Saints–*Jane Pusey & J. A. Pusey.* 1742 & 1753. By Peter Scheemakers (1691–1770) and his most successful
Berkshire monument. It is a large standing wall monument of veined marble with a reredos background. Scheemakers
exploits the motif of a seated female figure, cladding her in Roman dress. She reads a book and by her feet stands an urn.
Above, set in a roundel, is the bust of J. A. Pusey and the reredos is crowned by an open triangular pediment enclosing a
coat of arms. Each element is clearly expressed within the overall composition and decoration is kept to a minimum. It is
one of the best Georgian monuments in the county. Peter Scheemakers was the son of an Antwerp sculptor, who studied in
Denmark, went to Rome, and after a short stay came to England to work for Francis Bird. In 1728 he paid a return visit to
Rome coming back in 1735 with many models. As a sculptor, he ranks third behind Roubiliac and Rysbrack and it is
interesting to note that England's major sculptors of the mid-18th century were all foreigners. Scheemakers' son Thomas
(1740–1808) was also a sculptor. Other Berkshire monuments by the father are at Windsor (1735), Bray (1753) and Kintbury
(1754). Thomas' hand can be observed at Kintbury (1767).

70   RADLEY: St. James–*Sir William Stonhouse, his Wife & Son.* This large standing wall monument was made in 1633 by Nicholas Stone, the greatest sculptor of the Early Stuart decades. The tomb-chest with recumbent effigies and the son kneeling by his parents' head has a typical background with a coffered arch. Sir William and his wife's heads rest upon rich cushions and their son balances a skull upon his knee. The features are sensitively carved and so, indeed, are the hands, the latter very characteristic of Stone. But it is not at all an original work, rather an established type executed with a little more restraint than was usual. The kneelers along the tomb-chest are of a much poorer quality, and are no doubt the work of an assistant. Nicholas Stone (1586–1647) was born at Woodbury in Devon, the son of a quarryman. After a London apprenticeship he went to Holland where he worked for Hendrik de Keyser. He returned in 1613 bringing with him many new ideas gleaned from the wider vocabulary of the continent. Inigo Jones employed Stone on nearly all his buildings and the latter became King's Master Mason in 1632. His sculpture is the equivalent of Jones' architecture and it changed the whole course of English funerary monuments. Where his work is of a more conventional nature, the dictates of traditionally-minded patrons can be assumed.

71 & 72 RUSCOMBE: St. James. This is an important Carolean brick church, built 1638–39 and retaining a chancel of *c* 1200. The tower was built before the nave as it can be seen to cut into one of the tower buttresses. The most probable explanation is that a medieval tower collapsed or became dangerous, that this was rebuilt, and then a decision was taken immediately to rebuild a possibly dilapidated nave. The chancel was obviously in a better condition and so was not rebuilt. The photographs show (71) one of the nave windows and (72) the south porch. The former are most interesting. Not really Gothic Survival or Revival they can best be interpreted as a free variation on a medieval theme, an experiment often attempted by progressive church architects around 1900.

73 SHOTTESBROOKE: St. John Baptist–*Exterior from the East.* A splendid Decorated building, the church of a college established in 1337. Unaltered in every respect, Shottesbrooke remains a fortunate survival and a fitting companion to Early English Uffington (qv). Its spire is one of the landmarks of east Berkshire, a sleek, uncluttered structure without pretensions whose vertical emphasis is answered by the many fine elms scattered about the park. The church itself is a solid, comfortable cruciform building without frills, except for a certain play on window tracery. Buttresses against the chancel set up a happy rhythm, creating movement which complements the lively forms of the east window. The interior is impressively moving. There are few furnishings which results in a bareness that allows the architecture to speak forcibly. This is especially true of the chancel with its poignant monuments in brass and stone. They, the uncluttered stonework, the changelessness and the solitude create an emotional and visual experience to be remembered.

74 SHOTTESBROOKE: St. John Baptist–*The Chancel East Window. c*1337. One of the county's two major examples of flowing tracery, the other being at Warfield (qv). Here, the design is composed of the one basic motif, termed a mouchette. The effect is that of a tree branch or a butterfly. As there are no sub-arches the ensemble reads as one unit weaving to left and right of the central "stem". The forms are quite thin. A supple and extremely striking design.

75 SHOTTESBROOKE: St. John Baptist–*A Layman*. Late 14th century. One of the finest brasses in the county with two four-foot figures (the other is a priest) under tall crocketed ogee canopies. The priest wears vestments and the layman carries a sword. Both figures are exceptionally well designed, with the simple and firm treatment of the incised lines typical of early brasses. The design is linear and two-dimensional, executed without resort to shading which is the bane of so many late medieval brasses. Berkshire's earliest brass is at Wantage (a priest of *c*1330), the earliest knight is at Lambourn (1372), the earliest lady at Bray (1378). Altogether, the county preserves 127 medieval brasses (counting each individual figure).

76 SHOTTESBROOKE: St. John Baptist–*William Throkmorton*. 1535. William Throkmorton had the distinction of being the last warden of Shottesbrooke college. His monument is a very unusual and original one. He is represented lying in his coffin and across his waist is a stone band bearing a brass inscription. The effect is as if the lid had been removed exposing the dead figure inside. But Throkmorton is not commemorated by a cadaver, as one might have expected, but by the normal recumbent effigy with praying hands. The monument is of freestone.

77   SHRIVENHAM: St. Andrews–*The Arcades*. 1638. A rare and major example of a Carolean Gothic Survival church built around a pre-existing central tower. Inside, the arcades are composed of a mixture of Gothic and Classical elements. Tuscan columns, of excessive entasis, support round arches with medieval mouldings. It is a first-rate instance of a patron working within an old tradition but wishing to incorporate an up-to-date motif (in this case the columns). In spite of the columns, the church is entirely Gothic in spirit, with 'Perpendicular' windows. The interior is one of the most satisfying in Berkshire; cool, well lit and richly furnished with good woodwork.

78 SHRIVENHAM: St. Andrew – *The Pulpit*. 1638. An example of the forty-two Jacobean and Carolean pulpits in Berkshire. The main motif is a 'false perspective' panel set in each face, a three-dimensional conceit exploited also at Abingdon St. Helen and Buckland. Strapwork is prominent but arabesque is noticeably absent. Balusters at the corners. There is also a tester with pendants. Other dated pulpits are at Newbury (1607), Boxford (1618), Waltham St. Lawrence (1619), Hamstead Marshall (1622), Binfield (1628), Easthampstead (1631), Abingdon St. Helen (1636), Aldworth (1639) and West Hanney (1649).

79 SPARSHOLT: Holy Cross–*Detail of the North Doorway*. *c* 1190. A perfect illustration of the Transitional period's admixture of Romanesque and Gothic motifs, showing a round arch with a band of lobes and a roll moulding (i.e. Romanesque motifs but the roll thinner than the Normans would have made it). Still beasts' heads have been used as hood-mould stops. The capitals in the photograph are equally eloquent. The one on the left is of the waterleaf type, a design typical of *c* 1170–90. The other is an early form of stiff-leaf (ie. a Gothic type). Berkshire preserves forty-four Transitional doorways, not all as valuable as this one.

80 SPARSHOLT: Holy Cross–*Lady Achard.*
c 1353. There are about a hundred wooden
effigies in England and Berkshire is lucky
enough to possess six of them. Three are to be
found here at Sparsholt, lying amidst the deep
shadows of the south transept. They
commemorate Sir Robert Achard and his two
wives and rest upon three separate tomb-
chests, the ladies under recesses. The
knight's legs are uncrossed (which suits the
date). The effigies of his wives are very
beautiful figures with long vertical drapery
folds sweeping to one side at their feet. Both
have pillows supported by angels and one
wears a wimple (see the photograph). They
are amongst the finest effigies of any date in the
county, fitting occupants for one of Berkshire's
most rewarding churches. Oak effigies remain
also at Barkham, Burghfield and Englefield.

81   SUNNINGWELL: St. Leonard–*The Porch. c* 1560. A charming and rare example of Elizabethan church architecture. There was little need for new churches or even additions to churches after the Reformation. The Middle Ages bequeathed a legacy of well over ten thousand churches to the new Age of Humanism and many must have fallen into disuse and decay. Most counties can produce only a handful of examples of Elizabethan building. Fewer still can boast of features incorporating Renaissance motifs since most ecclesiastical work of the day was pure Gothic Survival. But here we see Ionic columns set on high pedestals employed to express the angles of the seven-sided porch. Instead of a parapet there is a heavy entablature. Yet the windows and doorway are still accurate Perpendicular. The porch may have been erected by Bishop Jewel of Salisbury, a former rector of Sunningwell.

82   SUTTON COURTENAY: All Saints–*Window in the Tower. c*1160–70. Sutton Courtenay possesses the only Norman tower of Berkshire, a stumpy structure heightened in the early 14th century. Its west window and the former bell-openings are the most interesting Norman windows in the county. The south bell-opening is illustrated, and shows two lights with a central shaft and intersecting arches, instead of the usual round head to each light. The shaft carries a trefoil-scallop capital, a Reading Abbey motif, and the jamb stones have been cut into a rough chevron (or zig-zag) pattern. The west bell-opening is identical; the west window below it is a single light with nook-shafts and a band of chevron (placed at right-angles to the wall) in the arch.

83   SUTTON COURTENAY: All Saints–*The South Porch*. Late 15th century. An exceedingly charming two-storeyed porch built of brick, the earliest occurrence of this material in a Berkshire church. In its own way, it can be called a secular rather than a religious piece, the kind of feature one might expect to find attached to a contemporary manor house. The porch is supported by diagonal buttresses of two set-offs, the doorway of which has a square hood-mould and quarterfoiled circles in the spandrels; and is lit by two-light windows. The contrast between the warm brick and the cool stone of the rest of the church is extremely effective as is the contrast of brickwork against green foliage.

84   SUTTON COURTENAY: All Saints–
Respond & Corbel in the South Aisle. c 1300
and *c* 1400 respectively. The respond belongs
to the south arcade but carries a re-set
Norman arch (the original chancel arch). The
aisle was added to an aisleless 12th century
church, using the old chancel arch as the east bay
of the arcade. Single-shafted respond with
moulded capital. About 1400 the aisle was rebuilt with large Perpendicular windows, two
image corbels being placed either side of the
east window. They would have carried statues
of the saints to whom the altar was dedicated.

85   THEALE: Holy Trinity–*Exterior from the South-East.* 1820–32 by Edward Garbett, the tower 1827–28 by John Buckler. One of the most important early 19th century Gothic Revival churches in England. At this time churches were invariably designed in thin lancet or late medieval styles, archaeologically incorrect and often unatmospheric. But Garbett went to Salisbury Cathedral, taking motifs and re-vamping them in his own way to produce this extremely single-minded building. The earlier 13th century had little popularity as a source of motifs, especially after Pugin and the Ecclesiologist had successfully pleaded for the Second Pointed, ie. the style of *c* 1250 to *c* 1320. At Theale the west front, the lancet windows and the buttresses are emphatically Salisbury. The building is very tall but also extremely long and the two emphases counteract each other. Necessary relief is provided by the tower which lends strength to the vertical at the expense of the horizontal. The interior has plaster rib vaults. Edward Garbett (died *c* 1825) was a local Reading architect, the son of William Garbett, surveyor to Winchester Cathedral.

86 TIDMARSH: St. Laurence–*The Apse. c*1230–40. This singular structure is the only polygonal 13th century apse in an English parish church. A few of the Decorated period exist but they can be explained as being derived from the Wells Lady Chapel and the Lichfield Choir. But there does not appear to be a direct precedent for Tidmarsh except that Pershore Abbey's choir ends in a polygonal apse on the French model. Pershore was consecrated in 1239. The English never liked the apse and the 13th century especially preferred square-ended plans. Perhaps the apse at Tidmarsh stands upon the foundations of a Saxon polygonal apse (cf. Wing in Buckinghamshire). Its windows are broad lancets and the interior was formerly rib-vaulted (now replaced by a plaster copy). The shafts with their "wind-blown" stiff-leaf capitals survive. The master mason may have come from an abbey or cathedral workshop, which could explain the originality of the design.

87 TIDMARSH: St. Laurence–*The South Doorway. c*1160–70. As the most accomplished Norman doorway in Berkshire and surely one of the finest in England, this has been executed with a control and sensitivity not characteristic of Norman abstract decoration. Three continuous orders enriched with beautiful bands of trailing, chain and chevron, all decorated with beading, and culminating in the head of Christ at the apex, comprise this beautiful work. It is an exceptionally noble and monumental design. Other worthwhile doorways of this period can be seen and enjoyed at Ashbury, Avington, Bucklebury, Chaddleworth, Lockinge, Padworth and West Hanney. Altogether, there are forty-three in the county.

88   UFFINGTON: St. Mary–*From the East.* A major Early English parish church of *c* 1250, major for England as well as for Berkshire, known locally as the Cathedral of the Vale. It incorporates several unusual features such as the octagonal crossing tower, the porch attached to the south transept and the shallow chapels off the transepts. Externally, the building is almost symmetrical in its general massing and impressively severe and single-minded. Only the two porches make a show but even there nothing is done to excess. Especially successful are the grouped lancets in transepts and chancel; the chancel is the best of its date in the county. It was meant to be vaulted but, regrettably, only the wall-shafts were completed. The nave is surprisingly bare and barn-like, sombre and static where the chancel is glowing and articulate. As regards architectural ambition and classicity, Uffington is unmatched by any other church in Berkshire. The plan is the one known as cruciform (four arms around a central tower), the most satisfying medieval church plan.

89   UFFINGTON: St. Mary–*The South Transept East Chapel. c*1250, altered *c*1678. These unusual chapels, two against the north transept and one against the south, appear to have been altered about 1677–79, though documentary evidence is lacking. The church-wardens' accounts for 1678 state that £101 was spent on repairs, including a new nave roof. The church is reported as being "long ruinous". Certainly, the west wall is of this date, a John Deene having been paid £25 to rebuild it. It is likely that the windows of each chapel were rebuilt at the same time, triangular heads being inserted in place of arches. Their overall impression is not uncharacteristic of 17th century Gothic Survival work. Conversely, they are not characteristic of genuine Early English design.

90   UFFINGTON: St. Mary–*The Porch to the South Transept. c* 1250. Porches into transepts are uncommon. Perhaps this one was connected to a priest's house or was used for processions. Its design is personal and also extremely interesting. It has a gable with a large sunk quarterfoil, bold and clear-cut, an almost semi-circular arch to the doorway and a pointed tunnel-vault inside. Thc latter motif is rare in England. Of the stone porches of Berkshire this is decidedly one of the most accomplished.

91   UFFINGTON: St. Mary–*Arcade to the North Transept Chapels. c* 1250. This arcade, and the single arch to the corresponding south transept chapel, represent the peak of Early English architecture in Berkshire. No other feature can quite match the sophisticated elegance displayed here. Beautifully detailed, richly moulded arches, and fine shafts carrying perfect moulded capitals make this feature memorable. Note that the bell of each capital is polygonal, not circular, something unexpected before the mid-14th century.

92   UFFINGTON: St. Mary–*Detail of the South Door. c*1250. A finely composed design with large C-shapes to the hinges and also symmetrical groups with tight, spring-like scrolls. The latter display leaf terminations. The only door which can compare with this is the earlier one at Faringdon (qv). There exists, however, an even finer door in St. George's Chapel, Windsor.

93 WALLINGFORD: St. Peter–*The Spire.*
1777. By Sir Robert Taylor (1714–88). Added to
a church built 1760–69. The spire, 109 feet high,
was originally designed for Long Ditton,
Surrey, but in the event never erected there.
It is a strange design, partly Classical and
partly Gothic. The drum or cupola is
octagonal with cinquecusped lights. The
spire has three bands of quarterfoils and
four tiers of lucarnes which do not project
vertically but keep to the slope of the spire.
The best view is from the bridge over the
River Thames. Taylor, the son of a stone-
mason, began as a sculptor, turning to architecture about 1753. He trained under
Sir Henry Cheere and visited Rome *c* 1743.
Returning penniless he built up a large
practice, almost monopolising the profession
during the mid-18th century. Architect to the
Bank of England and the Board of Works, he
was knighted in 1782 when Sheriff of London.
His style is Palladian, competent but
conservative. To see other examples of his ·
work in Berkshire one must step outside the
realms of church architecture (eg. Maiden-
head Bridge).

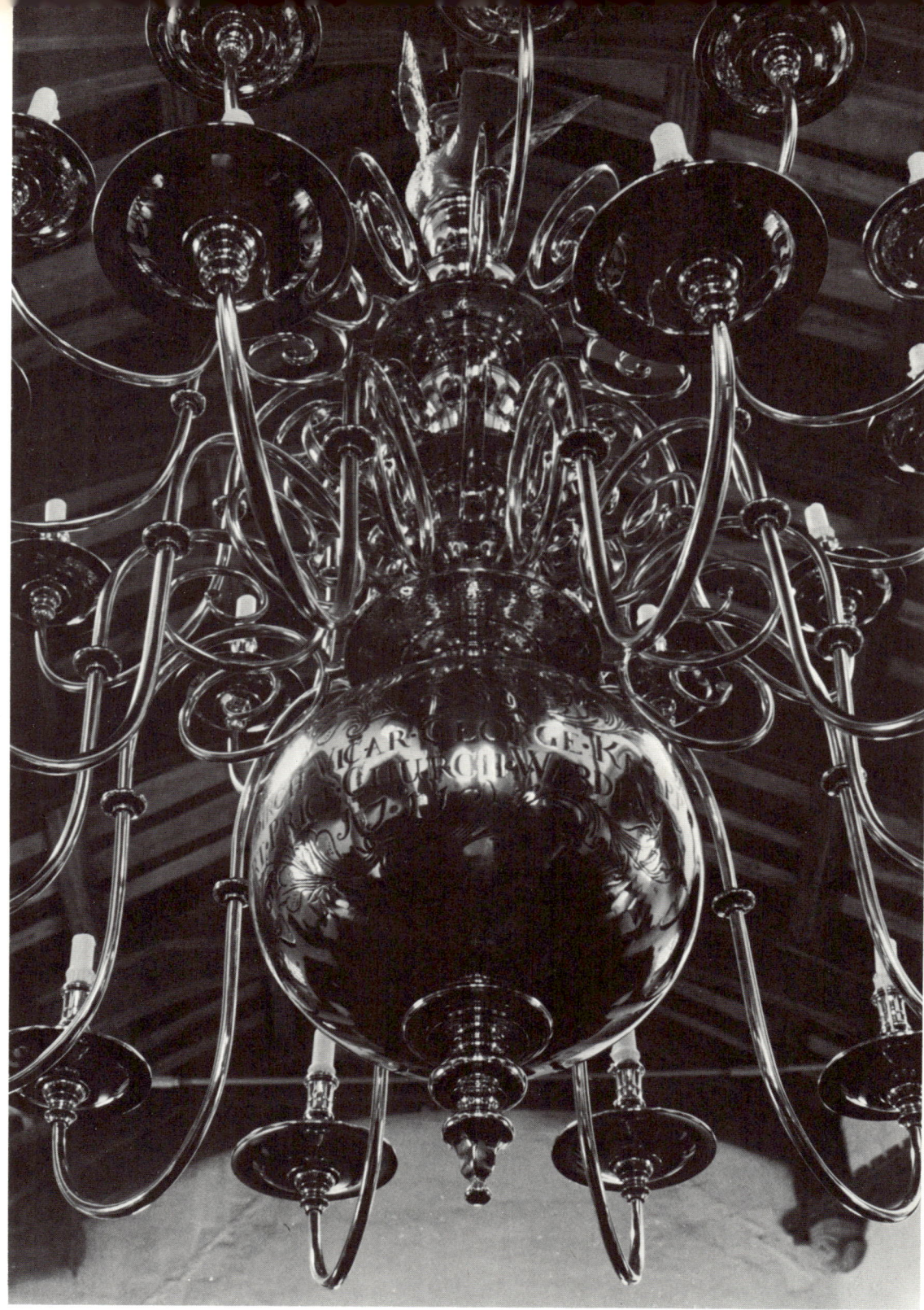

94 WANTAGE: St. Peter & St. Paul–*Chandelier*. 1711. This is the finest of Berkshire's sixteen brass chandeliers. They belong to a type of Dutch origin which was introduced into England during the reigns of the later Stuarts. The earliest example in our county is at Sonning (1675). Two varieties of bowl were usual, one circular as here, the other of a more Baroque shape. The Wantage chandelier possesses two tiers of "branches" but sometimes there could be three or often just one. Besides Sonning and Wantage, Abingdon St. Helen (1710 & 1713), Aldermaston (two, both 18th century), Brightwell (18th century), Buckland (two, both 1733), Caversham (1743), Harwell (1766), Shrivenham (1726), Little Coxwell (1729), Woolstone (1754), Wootton (18th century) and Sutton Courtenay (1821) preserve these elegant pieces.

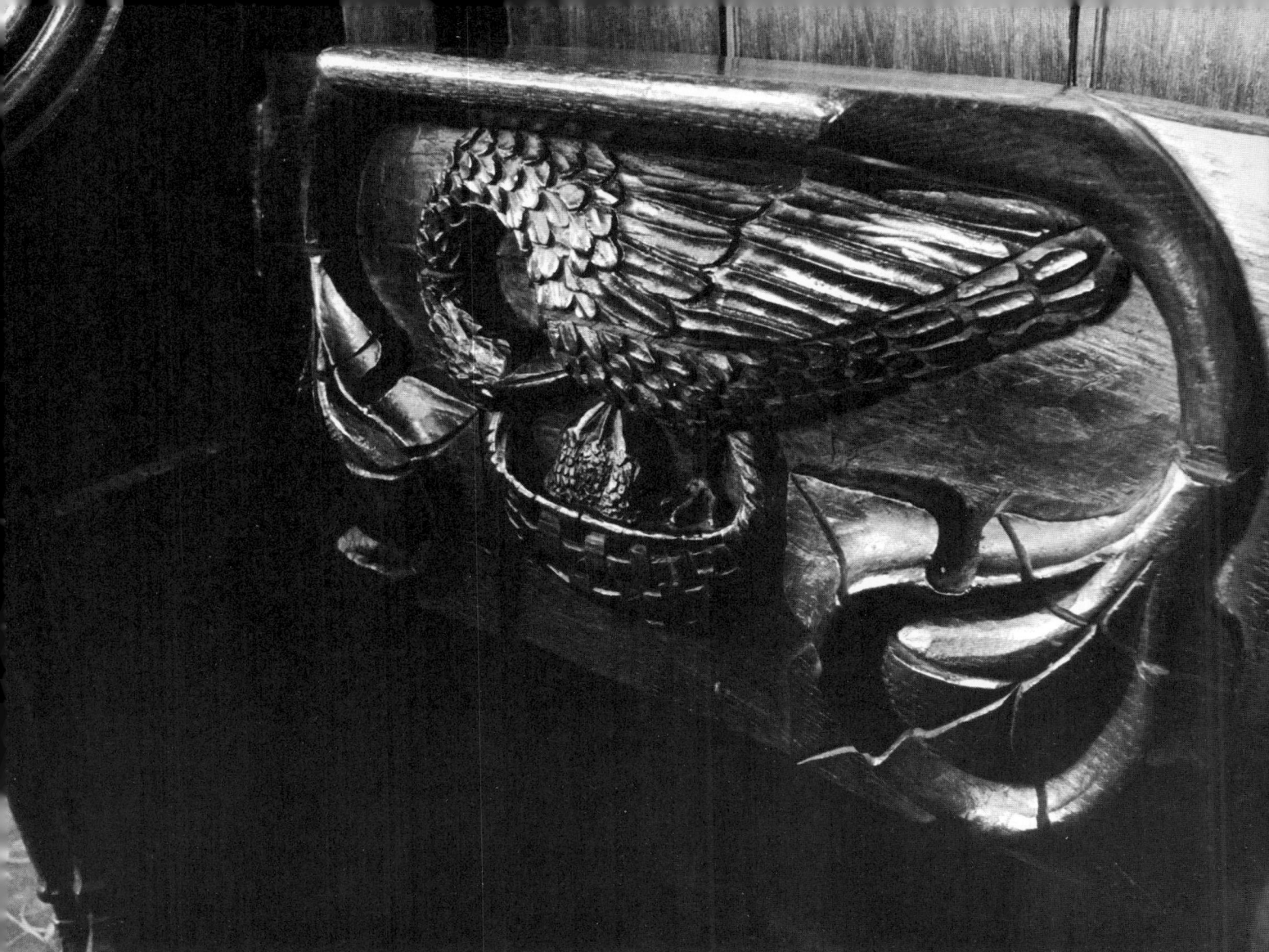

95　WANTAGE: St. Peter & St. Paul–*Misericord.*
c 1480. One of seventeen misericords attached
to the choir stalls, the only extensive set in the
county. That illustrated depicts the Pelican in
Her Piety, an allegory of Christ redeeming his
blood for Mankind. The bird feeds its young
with blood from its own breast. It is one of the
most popular subjects amongst a medieval
sculptor's or wood carver's repertoire. Another
misericord displays a double-headed eagle, a
third three flagons. The remainder bear shields
or leaf. Other churches with misericords are Radley (twelve of the 17th century)
and Sutton Courtenay (three of *c* 1300).

96　WARFIELD: St. Michael–*The North Aisle
Roof. c*1330. This, and the nave roof, are
amongst the stateliest examples of medieval
carpentry in Berkshire. They form a striking
feature of this fine church's interior, both
being identical in their construction. The sys-
tem includes tie-beams on curved braces,
collar beams on elegant sweeping curved
braces (almost arched braces in their
continuous flow) and wind-braces. The timbers
lack the mouldings often applied to later roofs.
About sixty pre-Perpendicular roofs survive in
the county, quite a surprising total.

97   WARFIELD: St. Michael–*The Screen.*
Early 15th century. An important piece,
notable for the preservation not only of its
roof-loft coving but of the loft itself, a rare
event anywhere. The arrangement of four-
light divisions, with tracery and sub-arches, is
also unusual for Berkshire. Indeed, in a county
of nondescript screens, Warfield is a major
work, though it would not stand out in Devon
or Norfolk. It has a panelled base with tracery,
and ribbed coving on shafts; the tracery is
particularly pretty above the lights, but that
of the loft west side is mainly restoration. Un
questionably, this is the finest Perpendicular
screen in Berkshire, proud and self-assured.

98   WARFIELD: St. Michael–*The Chancel East Window. c* 1330. The second of Berkshire's major pair of flowing tracery windows, it ought to be compared with that at Shottesbrooke (qv). Here the forms are much heavier and sub-arches split the composition into three units. The tracery is built around two motifs, viz. the mouchette and the quarterfoil, grouped into three independent sections. As a design it is less harmonious and more restless than Shottesbrooke.

99 WASING: St. Nicholas—*From the West.*
This small church, which preserves interesting
Georgian work, stands in a secluded, half-
forgotten churchyard near the centre of
Wasing Park. It is approached along a grassy
path that winds past ample hedgerows. The
nave, bell-turret and south transept date from
1761. The west porch is of a humble design and
has a pedimental gable. The weatherboarded
bell-turret is capped by a pyramid roof, and
rounded-arched windows filled with clear
glass light the nave. Happily, the Victorians
left the fabric alone although they carried out
internal alterations. The oldest features are
early 13th century and there is also work of
c 1280, *c* 1350 and *c* 1500.

100   WEST CHALLOW: St. Laurence–*The North Porch.* 15th century. Amongst the six timber porches of Berkshire, West Challow is unsurpassed. In addition, it rejoices in a healthy state of preservation. The doorway is framed by massive uprights weathered silver-grey and the roof is of lichen-patterned stone slates. The bargeboard is delightful with small-scale cusping and cusped panel motifs stepping up to the apex. The open sides, which rest upon a stone base, have moulded mullions with simple cusped arches between. One would have to search hard in any county to find such an attractive porch as this.

Glossary

The numbers indicate the photograph illustrating the term.

Addorsed figures: Figures arranged symmetrically back-to-back   35

Affronted figures: Figures arranged symmetrically front-to-front   4

Angle buttresses: Buttresses meeting at right-angles against the corner of a tower, etc.   47

Apse: Semi-circular or polygonal termination of a chancel, chapel, etc.   86

Arabesque: Light, incised or applied surface decoration consisting of flowing lines, flowers, etc.   63

Arcade: A sequence of arches carried on piers, either free-standing or set against a solid wall   8, 15, 25, 39, 40, 41, 77, 91

Ashlar: Blocks of masonry cut to even size and facing

Ballflower: Motif of the Decorated period consisting of a globular flower with three petals   67

Baluster: A small pillar, often carved, used to form the balustrade of a staircase, parapet, etc.   58, 64, 78

Bargeboard: Projecting decorated board placed against the incline of a gable to cover the joint between wall and roof   58 100

Capital: The uppermost member of a pier, respond, etc. Moulded or carved   4, 11, 23, 39, 40, 53, 60, 77, 79, 82, 84

Carolean: Historical division of English architecture covering the reigns of the Stuarts (except James I), ie. 1625 to 1689   19, 40, 71, 72, 77, 78

Censing: As of angels. Figures swinging incense jars   61

Chantry: A private chapel in which a priest daily recited a Mass for the deceased person's soul   67

Clerestory: The upper row of windows above an aisle   40, 65, 66

Coffered Arch: An arch decorated with sunken panels, each panel usually enclosing a flower, etc.   22, 70

Conceit: An artistic "trick of the trade". A device employed to exploit an effect, mood, etc.   78

Corbel: A projecting block, often carved, supporting a beam, arch, etc.   12, 22, 36, 41, 48, 84

Crocket: A decorative motif applied to gables, pinnacles, etc., usually of leaf form   8, 9, 10, 13, 66, 75

Crossing: The central space of a cruciform church consisting of four identical arches equal in dimensions to the nave, transepts and chancel   22, 39, 40, 41, 44, 58, 100

Cusp: The point between the foils in a trefoiled or cinquefoiled arch   8, 44, 58, 100

Decorated: Historical division of English architecture covering the period from *c.* 1280 to *c.* 1350   7, 8, 9, 10, 11, 13, 44, 46, 48, 49, 58, 59, 61, 67, 73, 74, 80, 84, 96, 97

Diagonal buttresses: Buttresses intersecting the right-angle of a tower, etc., ie. projecting diagonally   83

Early English: Historical division of English architecture covering the period from *c.* 1175 to *c.* 1280   14, 38, 42, 44, 47, 56, 60, 86, 88, 89, 90, 91, 92

Effigy: A sculptural representation of the human figure   5, 8, 9, 10, 18, 43, 52, 57, 61, 70, 76, 80

Entablature: The horizontal member of a Classical portico, etc., above the columns   3

Entasis: A convex curve applied to columns, etc., to counteract the optical illusion of concavity inherent in straight lines   77

Garland: Carved decoration in the form of a string of fruit, leaves, etc.   54

Georgian: Historical division of English architecture roughly corresponding to the reigns of the four Georges (1714–1830)   2, 24, 33, 68, 69, 93

Hood-mould: A projecting moulding above an arch designed to throw water clear of the window, etc., below. Also used internally   7, 49, 67, 79, 83

Iconography: The subject matter of the visual arts   12, 15, 26

Jacobean: Historical division of English architecture corresponding to the reign of James I (1603–1625)   19, 20, 25, 45, 63, 64

Jamb Stones: The stones forming the sides of an arch, doorway, etc.   82

Label stop: A figural or decorative block placed at each end of a hood-mould   7, 49

Medallion: A circular device containing a portrait or a scene   2

Misericord: A carved bracket underneath the tip-up seats of medieval choir stalls. Usually carved with figures, scenes, beasts, etc.   95

Modillion: A square bracket supporting a cornice in Classical buildings   3

Mullion: A vertical shaft dividing a window into separate lights   30, 59, 100

Nook-shaft: A thin shaft set into the angle of a pier, jamb, etc.   22, 47, 82

Ogee: A flowing line or curve, alternately convex and concave, struck from two opposing radii. Much used for arches during the Decorated period   58, 67, 75

Pediment: A motif of Classical architecture placed above a window, portico, etc. Similar to a low-pitched gable, it can be triangular or segmental   3, 99

Pendant: A roof boss elongated downwards   78

Perpendicular: Historical division of English architecture covering the period from *c.* 1330/50 to *c.* 1530   5, 6, 12, 27, 30, 31, 35, 36, 37, 43, 57, 65, 66, 83, 84, 95, 98, 100

Piscina: A basin set into a wall or sometimes projecting. Used by the priest for washing the Communion vessels   67

Poppyhead: A finial, usually in the form of leaves, decorating the tops of bench and stall ends   35

Portico: Centrepiece of a Classical building consisting of a pediment on columns   3

Rere-arch: The internal arch of a window or doorway   48

Reredos: A carved or painted background to an altar   37, 69

Respond: A half-column set into a wall and supporting one end of an arch   23, 41, 84

Rood-loft coving: Concave, fan-shaped feature above the tracery of a medieval screen, designed to support the floor of the rood-loft   98

Roundel: A circular niche containing a bust, relief, painting, etc.   69

Sedilia: Seats for the clergy recessed into the wall of the chancel and often placed under canopies   49

Shell Niche: A niche fashioned in imitation of a scallop shell   54

Shingles: Wooden tiles covering a roof or spire   31

Strapwork: A 16th century decorative motif consisting of interlacing flat bands resembling leather straps   18, 64, 78

String-course: A continuous horizontal moulding applied to a wall

Stucco: Finished plasterwork, usually laid over brickwork or occasionally wood   3

Sub-arches: Subsidiary arches below a main arch   59, 98

Tester: Flat canopy placed above a pulpit   78

Tie-beam: A horizontal beam in a timber roof, placed transversely at the height of the wall plate   31, 97

Touch: A black marble quarried near Tournai. Used for columns, etc., on 16th and 17th century monuments   19

Tracery: The ornamental infilling above the lights of a window. Also used as surface decoration   27, 30, 46, 47, 51, 56, 59, 73, 74, 96, 98

Transitional: Historical division of English architecture covering the period when Romanesque gave way to Gothic, ie. *c.* 1170 to *c.* 1200   22, 23, 28, 39, 40, 41, 62, 79

Triglyph: A decorative motif applied to the entablature of Classical buildings. A block with vertical grooves or mouldings   3

Tympanum: The solid infilling of an arch or doorway above the springing line   16, 26

Waterleaf: A large spreading leaf motif applied to capitals of the Transitional period   22, 39, 79

Weeper: A small figure placed against the sides of a medieval tomb   5, 6

Wind-braces: Arched timbers fixed to the rafters of a roof to withstand wind pressure   97

Bibliography

LOCAL

Bouchier, E. *Notes on Stained Glass of the Oxford District,* Blackwell 1918.

Clarke, B. & Colvin, H. *The Rebuilding of Berkshire Churches during the 17th, 18th & 19th centuries.* Berks Archaeological Journal (BAJ) Vol. 53 (1952–53).

Cole, F. *An Analysis of the Church of St. Mary, Cholsey,* Blackwell 1911.

Esdaile, A. 'English Sculpture in Some Berkshire Churches', BAJ Vol. 45 (1941).

Hallam, W. 'Baulking Church', Berks, Bucks & Oxon Arch. Journal (BBOAJ) Vol. 12 (1906).

Hallam, W. *History of the Parish of East Lockinge,* C. Bartlett 1900.

Howse, J. *Denchworth Through The Centuries,* J. House 1967.

Howse, J. *Goosey,* Vol. 2. J. House 1968.

Hurrey, J. *Reading Abbey,* Elliot Stock 1901.

Keyser, C. E. 'Articles on individual churches', BBOAJ Vols. 11–26 (1905–20).

Keyser, C. E. *The Norman Architecture of Berkshire,* Blacket, Turner (no date).

Keyser, C. E. 'Norman Doorways in Berkshire', BBOAJ Vol. 6 (1900).

Keyser, C. E. 'Notes on the Churches of the Lambourn Valley', BBOAJ Vol. 27 (1922).

Long, E. 'Mural Paintings in Berkshire Churches', BAJ Vol. 45 (1941).

Parker, J. *Ecclesiastical Topography of England: Berkshire,* Parker 1849.

Pevsner, N. *The Buildings of England: Berkshire,* Penguin 1966.

Preston, A. 'Fourteenth Century Painted Ceiling at St. Helen's, Abingdon', BAJ Vol. 40 (1936).

Preston, A. *St. Nicholas, Abingdon, & Other Papers,* Oxford Hist. Soc. 1935.

Sharpe, F. 'The Church Bells of Berkshire', BAJ Vol. 43 (1939).

Victoria County History: Berkshire, St. Catherine Press 1906–24.

Victoria County History: Hampshire, Vol. 4. St. Catherine Press.

Walker, J. 'Long Wittenham Church', BBOAJ Vol. 35 (1931).

Wethered, F. *St. Mary's Hurley in the Middle Ages,* Bedford Press 1898.

GENERAL

Boase, T. R. S. *English Art 1100–1216,* Oxford University Press 1953.

Caiger-Smith, A. *English Medieval Mural Paintings,* Clarendon Press 1963.

Clapham, A. *English Romanesque Architecture,* 2 Vols. Oxford University Press 1934.

Colvin, H. *Biographical Dictionary of English Architects 1660–1840,* John Murray 1954.

Evans, J. *English Art 1307-1461,* Oxford University Press 1949.

Gunnis, R. *Dictionary of British Sculptors 1660-1851,* Odhams n.d.

Pevsner, N. *An Outline of European Architecture,* Penguin 1963.

Remnant, G. L. *A Catalogue of Misericords in Great Britain,* Clarendon Press 1969.

Stone, L. *Sculpture in Britain: The Middle Ages,* Penguin 1955.

Summerson, J. *Architecture in Britain 1530–1830,* Penguin 1970.

Talbot-Rice, D. *English Art 871–1100,* Oxford University Press 1952.

Taylor, H. M. & Taylor, J. *Anglo-Saxon Architecture,* Cambridge University Press 1965.

Tristram, E. *English Medieval Wall Paintings: The 13th Century,* Oxford University Press 1950.

Woodforde, C. *English Stained & Painted Glass,* Clarendon Press 1954.